Astrology:

Understanding Zodiac Signs & Horoscopes To Improve Your Relationship Compatibility, Career & More!

Contents

Copyright

The History of Astrology and the 12 Zodiac signs

In modern day, the word astrology, according to encyclopedia Britannica, means the art and science of divining the future and fate of humans from indicators given by stars and other heavenly bodies. Historical evidence traces the origins of astrology to Babylon. The Babylonians learnt this age-old science and refined it over the time. The Greeks soon followed suit and embraced astrology. Early astrologists made charts, which they used to predict seasons of the year and recurrent celestial events of nature.

Astrology was primarily practical in bringing order in an otherwise chaotic situation at the time. The application of the field to predict weather for farmers was a later development. Astrology was also widely used to forecast catastrophes and war. Additionally, kings used the discipline to offer advice on future developments. This made early astrologers, to gain favor with the ruling elites of the time.

The term Zodiac is derived from Greek; it means a circle of animals. There are some suggestions that the discipline was invented in Egypt at the very onset although these are historical debates that have yet to be settled.

The zodiac is divided into 4 groups:

*The Fire Signs: Leo, Sagittarius, Aries

*Water signs: Pisces, Scorpio, Cancer

*Air signs: Libra, Aquarius, Gemini

*Earth signs: Virgo, Taurus, Capricorn

The above groups are inscribed on a circle in clusters referred to as houses. The divisions are based on the earth's daily rotation around the sun, and are linked to life matters such as relationships, finances, and travel.

The division of the 12 zodiac signs is in line with the earth's rotation around the sun for a year. Each planet as known at the time is associated with at least 2 signs; the sun and the moon control one sign a piece. The Babylonians believed that the sun and the moon, and five other planets (Jupiter, mars, Mercury, Saturn and Venus) possessed different powers. Mars, for instance was associated with aggression and war.

Horoscopes

The term horoscope is derived from Greek and means the map of the zodiac signs with the earth at the center. The Horoscope shows the relative position of the sun, moon, and planets at specific times of reference, e.g. the date of birth of an individual. It is worth noting that the times referred to in horoscopes do not follow the conventional clock. Rather, they are time as referred to the sidereal time; i.e. the time based on equinox.

Horoscopes are both meticulous and methodical and use charts and table listings (referred to as ephemeris) which can only be read and interpreted by skilled and experienced astrologers since, they require a meticulous eye to read the indicators accurately.

Astrology, as mentioned earlier, was supported and given new impetus by some great names of olden times. Philosophers such as Plato, Aristotle, Copernicus, Sir Isaac Newton, and Flamstead were open advocates of astrology. In more recent time, astrology has been supported by some famous public figures in society. One such figure is Nancy Reagan, the wife of the former US president Ronald Reagan.

The following is a summary guide on the timeframes within which each of the 12 zodiac signs are defined and described.

* 21st March to April 19th: Aries

*20th April to May 20th: Taurus

*21st May to June 20th: Gemini

*21st June to July 22nd: Cancer

*23rd July to August 22nd: Leo

*23rd August to September 22nd: Virgo

*23rd September to October 22nd: Libra

*23rd October to November 21st: Scorpio

*22nd November to December 21st Sagittarius

* 22nd December to Jan 19th: Capricorn

*20th Jan to Feb 18th: Aquarius

* 19th February to March 20th: Pisces

Profiles of the 12 Zodiac signs are as laid out in the various chapters below:

Aries

Symbol: The ram (dragon- Chinese symbol)

Element: Fire

Group: Emotional

Polarity: Positive

Opposite sign: Libra

Ruling planet: Mars

Chinese counterpart: dragon

House: 1st

Lucky gem: Diamond

Favorable color: Red

Personality

You are an energetic and boisterous person. You are also dynamic and competitive. Generally, you like to take the lead in everything. However, your weakness lies in being impatient and a tendency to be argumentative.

Relationship compatibility

Aries and Aries

This is an incompatible pair. The intention to dominate is too strong to sustain the relationship.

Aries and Taurus

Although it may seem blissful, this relationship is unlikely to go any further than the initial excitement. It can only be sustainable for the short term.

Aries and Cancer

The only thing that sparks a union here is sex. Unfortunately, there is little beyond the sexual attraction. Sex soon fades and leaves the pair with little else in common.

Aries and Libra

You are attracted to each other because of the mutual supply of what the other lacks. Demanding sexual intrigues may spoil the party for Libra though. You are unlikely to bond for long, even though the physical attraction is quite strong.

Aries and Leo

You are an exciting pair, given the amount of energy that you two exude. You are aggressive, filled with ego and always keen to steal the limelight. If you take a little time to study your strengths and weaknesses, you could pull a surprise and forge a lasting union.

Aries and Virgo

This pair differs sexually. This is a bad start for both; hence, a union is unlikely to succeed. Actually, it is a 50/50 game of chance.

Aries and Scorpio

Sex life could go either way; good or bad. It is an unstable relationship because you are both too independent to form a union.

Aries and Sagittarius

Since the temperament of these two match, a union has a great chance of succeeding.

Aries and Capricorn

This is a union bound to fail because of the tendency for both to want to dominate. Aries is also too extravagant for Capricorn's taste.

Aries and Aquarius

This is likely to be a stormy relationship but has a chance to work if you use some tact.

Aries and Pisces

This forms a complicated pair doomed to fail because fire and water do not mix.

Fitness, Diet and Health

Aries has a strong body formation with well-developed muscles and seldom worries about problems of being overweight. It is advisable that you eat more of proteins, so as to maintain your physique and energy needs. Eat more red meat, and eggs. Thyme and Ginseng are good additions to your diet.

Business

You thrive more on commission-based deals. Your best careers include soldier, police officer, firefighter, entrepreneur, TV, government, and politics.

Taurus

Symbol: The bull

Element: Earth

Group: Emotional

Polarity: Negative

Opposite sign: Scorpio

Ruling planet: Venus

Chinese counterpart: Snake

House: 2nd

Lucky gem: Emerald

Favorable color: Pink

Personality

You are a reliable and practical person. You like predictability and have a knack for music. You like such activities as gardening, cooking, and others that you can perform with your hands.

Your weakness is that you are possessive, stubborn, and uncompromising.

Relationship compatibility

Taurus and Aries

Although it may seem blissful, this relationship is unlikely to go any further than the initial excitement. It is only sustainable in the short term.

Taurus and Cancer

The relationship has a chance of working because you both need security and love, which you provide to each other.

Taurus and Libra

These two may work but have a slim chance of forming a lasting union.

Taurus and Capricorn

Capricorn and Taurus both love to work and will relish the money you make; you're your sweat. This combination is compatible.

Taurus and Taurus

This is a questionable union, as you fail to pay attention to each other.

Taurus and Gemini

Gemini is too changeable for Taurus; hence the relationship is bound to fail.

Taurus and Leo

There is a musical attraction but there are too many distractions for the relationship to work.

Taurus and Virgo

Even though you have a few sexual preference differences, you can still work to make a lasting relationship.

Taurus and Scorpio

You have a strong sexual attraction; hence, a union is likely to succeed, with a little tolerance.

Taurus and Sagittarius

This relationship is short-lived, as you have differing personalities that don't agree.

Taurus and Aquarius

Aquarius views Taurus as over-demanding; hence, this is likely to be a troubled relationship.

Taurus and Pisces

You form a compatible dreaming pair.

Fitness, Diet and Health

You are endowed with a resistant body. It is advisable that you eat bulgur, whole grains, and quinoa. Fenugreek is an especially great spice for you. Ensure that you avoid sugars as much as possible.

Business

You will excel as a media person, public speaker, chef, landscaper, lawyer, engineer, or educator.

Gemini

Symbol: Twins (horse- the Chinese counterpart)

Element: Emotional

Group: Positive

Favorable colors: Green

Ruling planet: Mercury

House: 3rd

Opposite sign: Sagittarius

Lucky gem: Agate

Personality

Gemini expresses a duality personality. You are expressive, quick witted and often flip flop between being extroverts, contemplative and serious.

Relationship Compatibility

Gemini and Leo

This is a relationship full of affection. It stands a good chance of sustaining a long term union. It is a safe marriage. Gemini appreciates the exuberance of Leo, while Leo is intrigued by the thoughtfulness of Gemini.

Gemini and Aries

This form a delightful and successful union. You are both active and keep searching for new knowledge and your sexual energy serves to seal the union deal.

Gemini and Libra

This functional union grows to bliss in the right environment. It is a very passionate union and is a perfect fit for both short and long-term unions.

Gemini and Taurus

This is an incompatible union and is bound to fail because Gemini is too outgoing and changeable for Taurus' taste.

Gemini and Scorpio

Your approach to life differs a great deal. You are incompatible, as Gemini is always doubting and outgoing while Scorpio is purposeful and jealous.

Gemini and Aquarius

You can unite successfully because each has an element of surprise and intrigue in them; a quality you both admire and live by literally, especially Gemini.

Gemini and Capricorn

This is an incompatible pair. Gemini is too outgoing and flirtatious for Capricorn. Although you are attracted sexually, other complications dull your great moments.

Gemini and Gemini

This is a sibling-like pair. You can form an unbreakable relationship and can display a crazy attraction and mad love life.

Gemini and Virgo

This union is short-lived since Gemini cannot cope with Virgos ways. Gemini finds Virgo too boring for life.

Gemini and Sagittarius

You display a strong sexual attraction but your relationship is short lived. Any attempt at a lasting union needs a lot of effort on both sides.

Gemini and Pisces

Gemini is a light-hearted outgoing partner. Pisces, on the other hand is too serious resulting in an unhappy union.

Gemini and Cancer

Gemini is too jumpy for Cancer who prefers to stay at home.

Gemini and Aquarius

You are compatible. Aquarius is just as unpredictable, which adds value to your relationship.

Fitness, Health and Diet

Gemini is prone to respiratory ailments, which manifest in narrow bronchiole tubes. It is advisable to eat fresh fruits, capriccios, fish, and vegetables. Your secret solution for your respiratory conditions is rosemary.

Business and Career Prospects

Gemini thrives in such careers as teaching, technical assistant, rescue workers, machine operator, and stock broking.

Cancer

Symbol: Crab

Element: Water

Group: Emotional

Polarity: Negative

Opposite sign: Capricorn

Ruling planet: Moon

Chinese counterpart: Snake

House: 2nd

Lucky gem: Pearls

Favorable color: White and Silver

Personality

You are an intuitive and sentimental person. You love being close to family and people you are familiar with. You are also a very emotional being and express lots of sympathy for others. Your weakness is the fact that you tend to cling to the past too much. You are also manipulative and prone to conflicts.

Relationship Compatibility

Cancer and Aries

This is a difficult match. Cancer's homebound ways will bore Aries.

Cancer and Taurus

This relationship has a chance of working because you both need security and love, which you can provide to each other.

Cancer and Gemini

Gemini is too jumpy for Cancer who prefers to stay at home.

Cancer and Cancer

The similarity makes this pair incompatible; too moody.

Cancer and Leo

Leo is able to stabilize moody cancer; hence, the relationship has a good chance.

Cancer and Libra

This union is incompatible. Libra can't stand Cancer's emotional changeability.

Cancer and Virgo

You are likely to form a lasting union because your personalities merge. However, Virgo needs to adjust a little.

Cancer and Scorpio

You form a compatible pair, as Scorpio provides what Cancer needs.

Cancer and Sagittarius

The personalities of these two differ to the extent of incompatibility since Sagittarius likes to go while cancer prefers the safety of home.

Cancer and Capricorn

You are both too sensitive to trivialities. Your union may last but it will be a boring and undesirable relationship.

Cancer and Aquarius

The marriage between you is a bad gamble. Aquarius complicates life for Cancer.

Cancer and Pisces

You are a compatible pair with lots of action in bed.

Fitness, Diet and Health

You are highly emotional. It is advisable that you eat more avocado, artichoke, fish, and fennel.

It would be best to use spices like caraway and coriander.

Business

You can make a good gardener, lawyer, soldier, teacher, or social worker,

Leo

Symbol: Lion

Element: Fire

Group: Intellectual

Polarity: Positive

Opposite sign: Aquarius

Ruling planet: Sun

Chinese counterpart: Monkey

House: 5th

Lucky gem: Ruby

Favorable color: Gold, orange

Personality

You have a knack for the dramatic. You are a pleasant person, attractive, charismatic, and creative. You are also outgoing and generally enjoy being in the limelight. In addition, you tend to pull others to you.

Relationship Compatibility

Leo and Scorpio

You enjoy a mutual sexual attraction. Your relationship has a good chance of succeeding. However, you need to guard against your tendency to be too strong willed.

Leo and Virgo

There is a good chance of a successful relationship. Virgo is overcritical but Leo can overlook it.

Leo and Gemini

This is a relationship full of affection. It stands a good chance of a sustaining long-term union, as Gemini appreciates the exuberance of Leo, while Leo is intrigued by the thoughtfulness of Gemini.

Leo and Capricorn

This relationship is rocky and is likely to fail. Leo is exuberant and exhibitionist while Capricorn is reserved and careful preferring stability.

Leo and Aries

You are an exciting pair, given the amount of energy that you two exude. You are aggressive, filled with ego and always keen to steal the limelight. None of you is willing to accept relegation to second place. Interestingly though, there is a steamy sex life between you. If you take a little time to study your strengths and weaknesses, you could pull a surprise and forge a lasting union. You only need skillful navigation to make it through.

Leo and Cancer

Leo is able to stabilize moody cancer; hence, the relationship has a good chance.

Leo and Libra

You are a compatible pair with a lot of sexual energy and indeed attraction. Your performance adds value to your relationship.

Leo and Taurus

There is a musical attraction but there are too many distractions for the relationship to work.

Leo and Leo

Your relationship is based on chance. It could work or fail. Selfishness is your greatest enemy.

Leo and Sagittarius

Your chance of forming a successful union is realistic. Your sex drive is your greatest relationship asset.

Leo and Aquarius

Aquarius doesn't want to be ruled. Leo can't get cooperation from Aquarius; thus, this is an improbable union, as differences suffice.

Leo and Pisces

Leo can't understand Pisces. You are simply mysterious to each other; thus the relationship cannot hold for long.

Fitness, Diet and Health

You are prone to hypertension. Therefore, watch out habits that could increase your chances of developing it. Avoid menus with caviar-champagne.

Use more olive oil and foods rich in iron. Saffron, marinades, and grilled meat are recommended diet options for you.

Business

You will do well as a tour guide, real estate agent, fashion designer, sales person, or interior decorator

Virgo

Symbol: The virgin

Element: Earth

Group: Intellectual

Polarity: Negative

Opposite sign: Pisces

Ruling planet: Mercury

Chinese counterpart: Rooster

House: 6th

Lucky gem: Sardonyx

Favorable color: Green and brown

Personality

You have a strong tendency to pay a lot of attention to detail. You are humane, analytical, gentle but also delicate.

On the flip side, you should watch against your tendency to be a workaholic. Avoid being overcritical.

Relationship Compatibility

Virgo and Leo

There is a good chance of a successful relationship. Virgo is overcritical but Leo can overlook it.

Virgo and Aries

This pair differs sexually. This is a bad start for both of you; hence, a union is unlikely to succeed because Virgo is also critical and fussy.

Virgo and Cancer

You are likely to form a lasting union because your personalities merge. However, Virgo needs to adjust a little.

Virgo and Libra

Virgo likes money while Libra likes sex. These divergent interests complicate your relationship; hence this relationship is unlikely to hold for long.

Virgo and Taurus

Even though you have a few sexual preference differences, you can still work to make a lasting relationship.

Virgo and Scorpio

This union won't last as you differ greatly in the sex department.

Virgo and Aquarius

There is no sexual attraction; hence, the relationship is unlikely to last.

Virgo and Capricorn

They form a compatible pair. Their personalities merge comfortably. Marriage is more likely to succeed.

Virgo and Gemini

This union is short-lived. Gemini cannot cope with Virgos ways, since Gemini finds Virgo too boring for life.

Virgo and Virgo

If you can consciously work to reduce your natural tendency to be overcritical, you could form a lasting union.

Virgo and Sagittarius

You have a distinctly different approach to life. Sagittarius enjoys sex and is hot while Virgo is busy with other life matters.

Virgo and Pisces

This pair is unlikely to succeed in a relationship, as Pisces is emotional and sensual while Virgo doesn't pay much attention to sex.

Fitness, Diet and Health

You have a liking for being slim and look healthy. Make sure you eat at regular hours and eat more fruits and vegetable: beans and legumes, cauliflower and celery, apricots, pomegranates.

Business

You stand a good chance of making money from teaching, being an editor, detective, statistician, translator, or writer.

Libra

Symbol: The scales

Element: Air

Group: Intellectual

Polarity: Positive

Opposite sign: Aries

Ruling planet: Venus

Chinese counterpart: Dog

House: 7th

Lucky gem: Sapphire

Favorable color: Blue

Personality

You have a well-balanced and peaceful personality. You also like to share what you have, and are drawn to harmony and gentleness. You are also gracious and fair-minded although your weakness is that you tend to keep grudges and can be quite indecisive.

Relationship compatibility

Libra and Aries

You are attracted to each other because of the mutual supply of what the other lacks. Demanding sexual intrigues may spoil the party for Libra though; hence you are unlikely to bond for long even though the physical attraction is quite strong.

Libra and Taurus

While you may enjoy each other's company, you have a slim chance of forming a lasting union.

Libra and Gemini

This functional union grows to bliss in the right environment. It is a very passionate union and is a perfect fit for both short and long-term unions.

Libra and Cancer

This union is incompatible. Libra can't stand Cancer's emotional changeability.

Libra and Leo

You are a compatible pair with a lot of sexual energy and indeed attraction. Your performance adds value to your relationship.

Libra and Virgo

Virgo likes money while Libra likes sex. Divergent interests complicate your relationship; hence, it is unlikely to hold for long.

Libra and Libra

Your marriage is bound to be a laborious one, as you are too demanding for each other.

Libra and Scorpio

Scorpio is too dangerous for Libra's free spirit and care-freeness about sex.

Libra and Sagittarius

This pair is compatible and stands a chance of succeeding in a marriage. Libra excites Sagittarius sexually and Sagittarius is full of adventure.

Libra and Capricorn

Capricorns busy ways will ruin the relationship even though you are initially sexually attracted. In addition, Capricorn thinks Libra is lazy.

Libra and Aquarius

You are compatible.

Libra and Pisces

Pisces is too sulky for Libra; hence, the union won't work.

Fitness, diet and health

You are slim figured.

It is important that you pay more attention to your kidneys, as you are easily affected by crisis situations. It is also advisable to eat food with lots of fiber to guard you against stomach complications such as constipation due to emotional upsets. You should also eat plenty of vegetables, fruits, pepper, and mint.

Business

You can make a good diplomat, scientist, dancer, salesperson, travel agent, host or negotiator.

Scorpio

Symbol: Scorpion

Element: Water

Group: Intellectual

Polarity: Negative

Opposite sign: Taurus

Ruling planet: Pluto, Mars

Chinese counterpart: Pig

House: 8th

Lucky gem: Opal

Favorable Color: Dark Reds, Black

Personality

You exude a determined personality. You are passionate about what you do, have plenty of energy, and are a very resourceful person. You are brave and friendly to people making it is easy for you to form connections with others.

Relationship compatibility

Scorpio and Leo

You enjoy a mutual sexual attraction. Your relationship has a good chance of succeeding. Guard against your tendency to be too strong willed.

Scorpio and Aries

Your sex life could go either way, good or bad. This is an unstable relationship as you are both too independent to form a union.

Scorpio and Cancer

You form a compatible pair, as Scorpio provides what Cancer needs.

Scorpio and Libra

Scorpio is too dangerous for Libra's free spirit and care-freeness about sex.

Scorpio and Taurus

You have a strong sexual attraction; hence, a union is likely to succeed, with a little tolerance.

Scorpio and Capricorn

You are sexually compatible, as Capricorn finds security in Scorpio.

Scorpio and Gemini

Your approach to life differs a great deal. You are incompatible. Gemini is always doubting and outgoing while Scorpio is purposeful and jealous.

Scorpio and Virgo

The union won't last, as you differ greatly in the sex department.

Scorpio and Scorpio

Your Relationship is too stormy to Survive

Scorpio and Sagittarius

Sagittarius is likely to take off. Scorpio is too intense for Sagittarius.

Scorpio and Aquarius

Scorpio is too jealous while Aquarius is too moody; hence the relationship won't last.

Scorpio and Pisces

This union will last, since Scorpio likes the dependency of Pisces and Pisces feels loved

Fitness, Diet and Health

You are prone to constipation; therefore, you should eat foods with fiber. You should also ensure you consume lots of energy foods, pumpkin, seed oil, and evening primrose.

Business

Make your money from being a scientist, surgeon, lawyer, detective, physicist, or educator.

Sagittarius

Symbol: Archer

Element: Fire

Group: Theoretical

Polarity: Positive

Opposite sign: Gemini

Ruling planet: Jupiter

Chinese Counterpart: Rat

House: 9th

Lucky gem: Topaz

Favorable Color: Purple

Personality

You are an energetic and broad-minded person, an extrovert who likes travelling. You have a knack for finding out although your inquisitive ways can be an issue for others. Your have a sense of humor, generosity, and idealistic tastes. Additionally, you do not promise what you can't deliver.

Relationship compatibility

Sagittarius and Aries

Since your temperament matches, this union has a great chance of succeeding.

Sagittarius and Taurus

This relationship is short-lived, as you both come with personalities that don't agree.

Sagittarius and Gemini

You display a strong sexual attraction but your relationship is short lived. Any attempt at a lasting union needs a lot of effort on both sides.

Sagittarius and Cancer

Your personalities differ to the extent of incompatibility. Sagittarius likes to go while cancer prefers the safety of home.

Sagittarius and Leo

Your chance of forming a successful union is realistic. Your sex drives is your greatest relationship asset.

Sagittarius and Virgo

You have a distinctly different approach to life. Sagittarius enjoys sex and is hot while Virgo is busy with other life matters.

Sagittarius and Libra

This pair is compatible and stands a chance of succeeding in a marriage. Libra excites Sagittarius sexually while Sagittarius is full of adventure.

Sagittarius and Scorpio

Sagittarius is likely to take off as Scorpio is too intense for Sagittarius.

Sagittarius and Sagittarius

This union is unlikely to last. You are too unpredictable.

Sagittarius and Capricorn

You are incompatible because you have peculiar and unique sex habits that do not flow along.

Sagittarius and Aquarius

You are compatible and innovative in love and in bed. Try to give each other space, as your union has a high chance of succeeding

Sagittarius and Pisces

Your connection is sexually steamy but that's all.

Fitness, Diet and Health

Eat at frequent intervals. Also, consume more sushi, algae (Japan). Try to avoid cream sugar and salt in large amounts.

Business

You can make a great minister, editor, animal trainer, PR official or travel agent.

Capricorn

Symbol: Goat

Element: Earth

Group: Theoretical

Polarity: Negative

Opposite sign: Cancer

Ruling planet: Saturn

Chinese counterpart: Ox

House: 10th

Lucky gem: Onyx

Favorable Color: Brown

Personality

You are drawn to professionalism and traditional values. Generally, you are a disciplined person. Your weaker points include the fact that you tend to show a know-it-all attitude which does not augur well with others. You also tend to be pessimistic and unforgiving. The latter is a recipe for a troubled relationship.

Relationship compatibility

Capricorn and Aries

This is a union bound to fail due to the tendency for both to want to dominate. Aries is also too extravagant for Capricorn's taste

Capricorn and Taurus

Capricorn and Taurus both love to work and will relish the money they make from their sweat; hence you are compatible.

Capricorn and Gemini

This is an incompatible pair, as Gemini is too outgoing and flirtatious for Capricorn. While you are attracted sexually to each other, other complications dull your great moments.

Capricorn and Cancer

You are both too sensitive to trivialities. While your union may last, it will be a boring and undesirable relationship.

Capricorn and Leo

This relationship is rocky and is likely to fail because Leo is exuberant and exhibitionist while Capricorn is reserved and careful, and prefers stability.

Capricorn and Virgo

You form a compatible pair as your personalities merge comfortably. This means that your marriage is more likely to succeed.

Capricorn and Libra

Capricorn's busy ways will ruin the relationship even though you are initially sexually attracted. In addition, Capricorn thinks Libra is lazy.

Capricorn and Scorpio

You are sexually compatible, as Capricorn finds security in Scorpio.

Capricorn and Sagittarius

You are incompatible, as you have peculiar and unique sex habits that do not flow along.

Capricorn and Capricorn

This is a boring union, as there is nothing new.

Capricorn and Aquarius

The money spending ways of Aquarius will ruin the relationship. In addition, Capricorn is too conservative in bed.

Capricorn and Pisces

This union is compatible, as Capricorn likes to be admired and Pisces provides that.

Fitness, Diet and Health

You are strong and slim. Eat more phosphor and calcium, slow cooked foods, soups and sprouting seeds.

Business

You are more likely to excel as a banker, administrator, IT administrator, or scientist.

Aquarius

Symbol: Water

Element: Air

Group: Theoretical

Polarity: Positive

Opposite sign: Leo

Ruling planet: Uranus

Chinese counterpart: Tiger

House: 11th

Lucky gem: Turquoise

Favorable Color: Turquoise

Personality

You are a shy, energetic, eccentric, and boisterous person. You are excited with circumstances that require you to think, are the intellectual who is compassionate, intuitive, optimistic and objective.

Watch out against your natural tendency to be temperamental and hard to compromise.

Relationship compatibility

Aquarius and Capricorn

The money spending ways of Aquarius will ruin the relationship. Furthermore, Capricorn is too conservative in bed.

Aquarius and Aries

The relationship is a stormy one but has a chance to work if you apply some tact.

Aquarius and Cancer

The marriage between you is a bad gamble, as Aquarius complicates life for Cancer.

Aquarius and Libra

You are compatible.

Aquarius and Taurus

Aquarius views Taurus as over-demanding; hence, this is a troubled relationship.

Aquarius and Leo

Aquarius doesn't want to be ruled and Leo can't get cooperation from Aquarius. This is an improbable union.

Aquarius and Scorpio

Scorpio is too jealous while Aquarius is too moody; hence, the relationship won't last.

Aquarius and Gemini

You are compatible, as Aquarius is just as unpredictable, which adds value to your relationship.

Aquarius and Virgo

There is no sexual attraction. This union's success is hinged on sheer chance.

Aquarius and Sagittarius

You are compatible and innovative in love and in bed. Try to give each other space to increase the chances of your union succeeding.

Aquarius and Aquarius

You have good prospects for a successful union though you have a boring sex life.

Aquarius and Pisces

You are incompatible; hence, if you try a relationship, it is likely to end up in depression. This is because Pisces likes attention that Aquarius cannot provide.

Fitness, Diet and Health

Eat more ginger, herbs, and spices. Use detoxicants frequently, avoid excess meat, alcohol, and carbonated beverages

Business

You are likely to excel as a scientist, aviator, musician designer, organic farmer, and inventor

Pisces

Symbol: The fish

Element: Water

Group: Theoretical

Polarity: Negative

Opposite sign: Virgo

Ruling planet: Jupiter, Neptune

Chinese Counterpart: Rabbit

House: 12th

Lucky gem: Moonstone

Favorable Color: Lilac, Purple

Personality traits

You have a strong will in life. You are also an intuitive person, empathetic, creative, and insightful. In addition, music makes you feel calm and relaxed.

Your weakness is that you tend to be fearful and an escapist.

Relationship compatibility

Pisces and Sagittarius

Your connection is sexually steamy but that's all.

Pisces and Gemini

Gemini is a light-hearted outgoing partner. Pisces, on the other hand is too serious. This results in an unhappy union.

Pisces and Capricorn

This union is compatible because Capricorn likes to be admired.

Pisces and Aquarius

You are incompatible; hence, if you try a relationship, it is likely to end up in depression. This is because Pisces likes attention that Aquarius cannot supply.

Pisces and Scorpio

This union will last, as Scorpio likes the dependency of Pisces and Pisces feels loved

Pisces and Taurus

You form a compatible dreaming pair.

Pisces and Libra

Pisces is too sulky for Libra; hence, the union won't work.

Pisces and Cancer

You are a compatible pair with lots of action in bed.

Pisces and Aries

You form a complicated pair; hence, the union is doomed to fail. This is because fire and water does not mix.

Pisces and Leo

Leo can't understand Pisces; hence the relationship cannot hold for long.

Pisces and Virgo

This pair is unlikely to succeed in a relationship. Pisces is emotional and sensual; Virgo doesn't pay much attention to sex.

Pisces and Pisces

Your union is compatible. Your sympathetic qualities are complementary.

Fitness, Diet and Health

You experience slow metabolism. You also seem to be fond of seafood, which is okay but make sure you also eat more citrus fruits.

Business

You have a knack for art but you can also be a good nurse, veterinary officer, physiotherapist, artist, or philanthropist.

Free Daily Horoscopes

The following links will enable to you get free daily Horoscope:

http://www.yasminboland.com/#axzz3NXWXr1 ot

http://www.astrology.com/horoscopes

http://www.news.com.au/lifestyle/horoscopes

http://www.cainer.com.au/

Bonus Content!

As a token of our appreciation <u>Grand Reveur Publications</u> would like to give you access to our exclusive bonus content (including free eBooks!).

<u>**You're only a click away from receiving:**</u>

Exclusive pre-release access to our latest eBooks Free Grand Reveur eBooks during promotional periods

A method ANYONE can use to publish their own book and make passive income

<u>https://ignorelimits.leadpages.net/grandreveur publications/</u>

As this is a limited time offer it would be a shame to miss out, I recommend grabbing these bonuses before reading on.